This Is Our
HEART

A MINDFUL BOOK ABOUT LOVE

Kate Goodwin

This book is dedicated to Sister Ann Marshall who taught me the Connection between Mindfulness & the Holy Spirit

... And to Jordan, my fiancée

Here is a secret most people don't know,
The ENTIRE world...

...Is made up of HEARTS

Some people call them things like "atoms" or "molecules"

But really, they are tiny, sometimes invisible hearts.

Even with a strong microscope it looks like a circle but it is actually a heart

This is one of them zoomed in on a lot.

"♡"

Like this

So small that you cannot see them with a naked eye.

2

They are all around us!

We breathe them in on fresh sunny days
(and crisp winter ones too)

We smell them when Mom bakes fresh pizza

Arugala

We hear them when Elton John sings

And I guess that's why
they call it the blues...

We feel them when we pet soft kitties

Tim

And we taste them when we eat some
fine homemade cooking

mmm...

Thanks chef!

4

Once you realize this, You start to see hearts everywhere

And the whole world becomes a beautiful place!!

Then, if you are careful & kind...

And, if you pay close attention...

Magic can Happen!

Did you know...

Humans have the ability to actually CREATE

's?

It's true.

We call it...

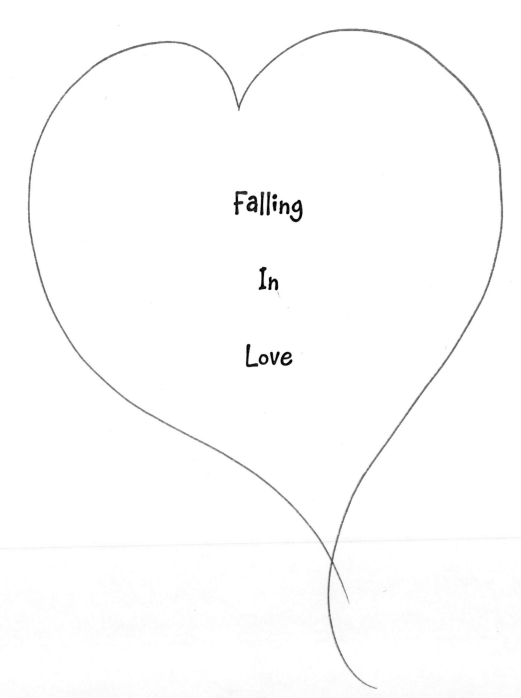

Falling

In

Love

Here is how it works:

When two people meet

Who find each other nice,

One tiny heart pops into existence.

When they share time together,

Attraction is formed,

And the tiny heart begins to grow.

When their eyes meet,

And they kiss,

The heart gets a bit stronger & brighter.

Now, there is no mistaking it,

A brand new heart exists,

And they can say...

This is our heart!

The best part about

Falling in Love

is Learning about

Your new heart

The more you talk to your new heart,

The more you learn about it.

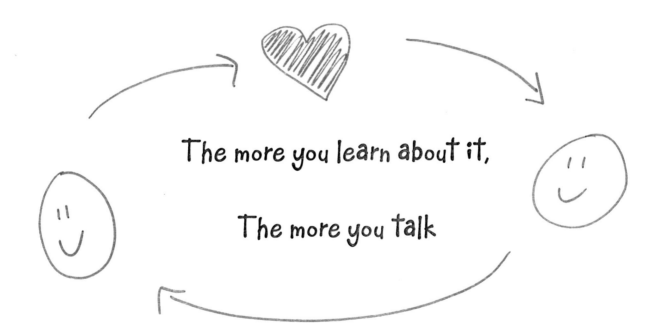

The more you learn about it,

The more you talk

Sometimes your heart makes you so excited

You want to dance.

Sometimes it makes you have

Sweet dreams

It makes you laugh on the phone,

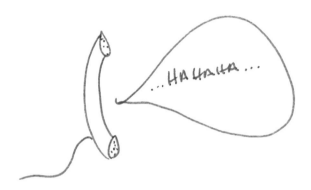

And makes you feel special & excited
& cared for & LOVED!

And then, all of a sudden this makes us scared!

What if our heart goes away?

What if one of us takes it, or breaks it?

What if our heart consumes us?

Or someone tries to be the boss of it?

What if one of us changes our mind or tries to own 51% of it?

What if our heart stops growing?

Or grows too fast?

What if...
What if...
What if...

What if it doesn't last?

Stop.

Breathe.

You can't see hearts

With thoughts

Like these.

Here is another secret most people don't know:
You are ALREADY a heart ♡

So, you can't become another one.

Which is meant to soothe your worries.
And remind you that
Your heart helps Our Heart,

that third member of this special trinity,
that mysterious energetic bond that keeps us together.

Here are some things we can do to care for Our Heart:

- Speak kindly

- Dance

- Cook

- Laugh

- Caress

- Sing

- Encourage

- Trust

- Be patient

- Teach

- Plant

- Move

- Honour &

LOVE

And if we can remember that there is nothing to be scared of, Our Heart will shine so big and bright that it will eclipse us currently and make us brand new.

And if it doesn't, we should remember...

...That it already has.